FIR

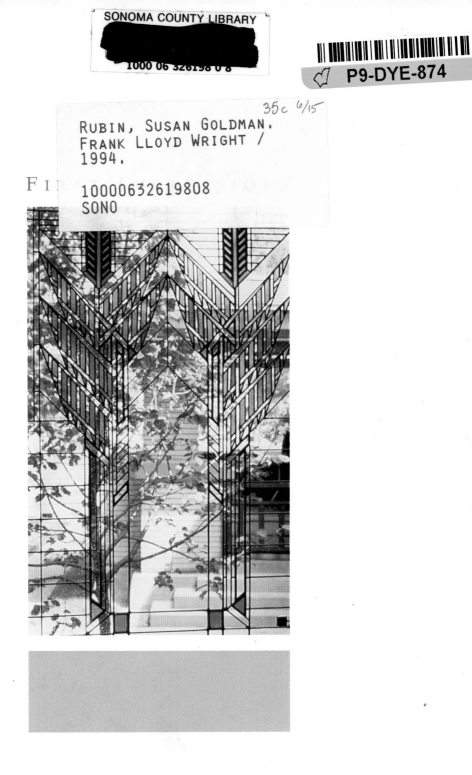

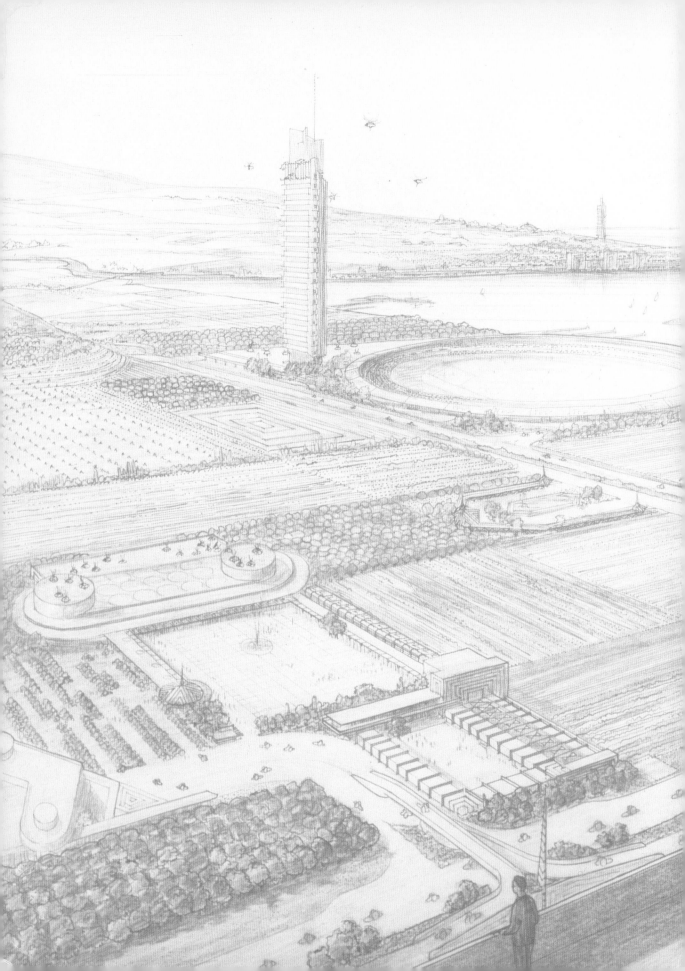

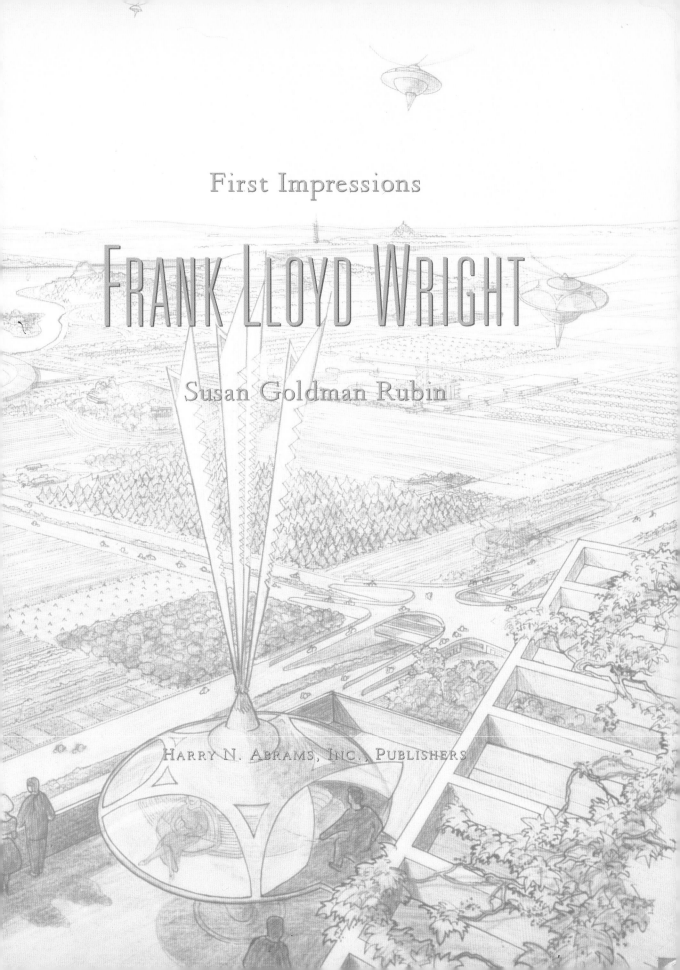

First Impressions

FRANK LLOYD WRIGHT

Susan Goldman Rubin

HARRY N. ABRAMS, INC., PUBLISHERS

For my son, Andrew, and my brother, Edwin P.
Moldof, and to the memory of Helen Hinckley Jones

This book was supported by a grant from the
National Endowment for the Humanities.

SERIES EDITOR: Robert Morton
EDITOR: Ellen Rosefsky
DESIGNER: Joan Lockhart
PHOTO RESEARCH: Jennifer Bright

Library of Congress Cataloging-in-Publication Data
Rubin, Susan Goldman.
Frank Lloyd Wright / Susan Goldman Rubin.
   p   cm.—(First Impressions)
Includes index.
ISBN 0-8109-3974-6
   1. Wright, Frank Lloyd, 1867–1959—Juvenile literature.
2. Architects—United States—Biography—Juvenile literature.
[1. Wright, Frank Lloyd, 1867–1959. 2. Architects.] I. Wright,
Frank Lloyd, 1867–1959. II. Title. III. Series: First impressions
(New York, N.Y.)
NA737.W7R83 1994
720'.92—dc20
[B]   93-48523

MASTER OF THE

WHEN FRANK LLOYD WRIGHT was eighty-nine, he designed a skyscraper one mile high. Although it was never actually built, it is just one example of his genius. Frank Lloyd Wright was a great American architect ahead of his time.

Wright conceived Mile High in a dream and woke up in the middle of

the night and made a quick sketch. Later that morning he went into his drafting room and drew a view of the building from the side (an elevation) and a small ground plan. Over the next few weeks, he redrew his conception of Mile High on a roll of canvas twenty-six feet long. He rendered it (adding tones of color) and then unveiled it for the press in a Chicago hotel

KNOW-HOW

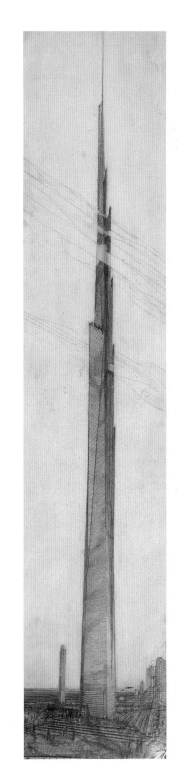

ballroom on Frank Lloyd Wright Day, September 17, 1956. Wright stood the painting against the wall. The blue sky in the background matched the color of the ballroom. As people stepped in, they felt as though they were seeing Mile High on the Chicago skyline.

Mile High was only one of many ideas Wright dreamed up. His imagination grew wilder as he grew older. Shortly before his death in 1959 when he was working on the Guggenheim Museum, he said, "A man slows down with age. It's inevitable." Wright was talking about other men, of course. "But I find it no drawback," he said. "I can do double, no, ten times the work I once could. Now I just shake the answer out of my sleeve. Every building is an experiment, but in the

(*Previous page*) FRANK LLOYD WRIGHT STANDS BESIDE A MODEL OF THE PRICE TOWER AT THE EXHIBITION "SIXTY YEARS OF LIVING ARCHITECTURE" IN 1953. BEHIND HIM IS A PHOTOGRAPH OF THE ARCHED ENTRANCE TO THE V. C. MORRIS SHOP IN SAN FRANCISCO.

(*Left*) WRIGHT'S CREATIVITY WAS AMAZING. IN THREE HOURS ONE MORNING HE DESIGNED THE MILE HIGH SKYSCRAPER, THE GREEK ORTHODOX CHURCH, AND THE BETH SHOLOM SYNAGOGUE.

same direction."

His sister Maginel, also an artist, asked him, "How do you do it? How do you think of it all?"

Wright answered, "I can't get it out fast enough."

During a career that lasted three quarters of a century, Wright continued to change and grow. Although he began practicing architecture in the late nineteenth century, his work still looks modern today. He thought about the place where a house would be built. Architects call this siting. Wright was unique in his love of the land in America. He used his imagination to create abstract architectural forms that echoed the natural shapes and rhythms of every setting he worked with. His genius was marrying each house or building to its environment. "The character of the site," he said, "is the beginning of the building. The good building makes the landscape more beautiful than it was before that building was built."

Wright's early "Prairie Houses," low and horizontal, suited the rolling midwestern landscape. His vertical cement block houses in southern California were dramatic extensions of the rugged hillside and took advantage of spectacular views. In his seventies, at an age when many people retire, Wright developed a different way of designing and explored curves and spirals. During this period he turned out some of his greatest masterpieces, such as "Fallingwater," a house built over a waterfall, and the Johnson Wax Administration Building, a work space that looked like a Hollywood set for a science-fiction movie.

THE LIVING ROOM AT WRIGHT'S HOME, TALIESIN, WISCONSIN, COMBINES OPEN AIRY SPACE WITH COZY NOOKS FOR READING AND PRIVATE CHATS. LIGHT POURS IN THROUGH HIGH CLERESTORY WINDOWS AND LOW WINDOW BANDS.

Fallingwater superbly harmonizes with its unusual wooded setting in every season of the year. It embodies the essence of shelter at its most artful: a cave, fixed in the rock, opens out to a lovely pavilion or building above the water. It has been called "a poet's dream" as well as "the realized dream of an engineer."

The Johnson Wax Administration Building demonstrates Wright's new interest in curves as a way of expressing something streamlined and inspirational in the workplace. Curved-glass tubing forms walls and domes. Light shimmers through the tubes. Lily pad or mushroom columns seem to float in the main workroom. Wright said of the building, "feel the freedom of *space.*"

One of Wright's most important contributions was to establish a new architecture appropriate to the American landscape and informal way of life. Rather than imitating and transplanting European styles the way most architects did and continue to do, he imagined new forms. He destroyed the usual boxlike arrangement of rooms and opened up interior space. The exteriors of

A GLASS TUNNEL OR BRIDGE
CONNECTS THE ORIGINAL
JOHNSON WAX ADMINISTRATION
BUILDING WITH THE RESEARCH
TOWER COMPLEX.

his building reflected his floor plans. Structure and ornament became integral parts of his designs. Wright based his designs on principles he called organic architecture. Nature inspired him; he wanted his houses to function as perfectly as a snail's shell. "Form and function are one," he once said.

To create a harmonious whole, Wright designed everything in the house or office building himself. He introduced many of the features we take for granted today such as built-in furniture, indirect lighting, split-levels (rooms slightly above or below adjoining rooms), and carports. He used natural materials—brick, stone, and wood—in their natural state, without paint, so they remained in their true form.

An attribute of his genius was that he thought in three dimensions; he envi-sioned a structure before drawing a sketch or elevation. Preliminary planning went on in his head, as it did when he designed the skyscraper Mile High. His son John, also an architect, remembered how his father planned Midway Gardens, an entertainment center for Chicago, in 1913:

I could not start my work until Dad determined the design. When a week rolled by I became worried, thinking that probably he was neglecting his work, but Dad said he was thinking it out and would have it shortly. And he did! One

morning he walked into the drafting room, up to my board, and rolled a clean sheet of white tracing paper on it.

"Here it is, John."

"Where is it?" I looked at the blank paper, puzzled.

"Watch it come out of this clean white sheet." Dad began to draw. The pencil

In Midway Gardens, created in 1914, Wright demonstrated all of his designing skills. For this indoor/outdoor dining, dancing, and entertainment center, he created the furniture, tableware, textiles, murals, and sculptures.

in his swift, sure hand moved rapidly, firmly, up, down, right, left, slantwise—mostly right and left. Within an hour, there it was! The exact dimensions, details, and ornamentation indicated by an interlocking organism of plans, elevations, sections, and small perspective sketches were all on the one sheet! The entire conception as to the design which was to cover a block square was completed. He drew balloons tied to the towers like the ones we played with at home. "There it is," he said. "Now get into it. Get it out." He laid down his pencil, picked up his stick, gave it a twirl, and sashayed out of the door.

Over the years Wright designed about one thousand structures, nearly half of which were actually built—an extraordinary record for a single architect. When asked which building was his greatest, he answered, "The next one . . . always the next one."

Not only was Wright a great architect but he was also a superb draftsman. Throughout his life he loved to draw. His wide range of interests included designing furniture, textiles, and decorative art glass, inventing (the wall-hung toilet remained one of his proudest accomplishments), playing the piano, writing, lecturing, farming, and collecting Japanese prints.

Yet above all, architecture mattered most to him. "It is basic," Wright said, "because we live with it." Architecture is an art form that people use. In designing a house an architect responds to what people need. How many will live in the house? What activities will go on there? How should the rooms be arranged? If a house is well designed, the people should live in it comfortably and feel protected, the way the architect intended. When an architect does an outstanding job of designing, the house also offers aesthetic pleasure—it is beautiful. In Frank Lloyd Wright's hands architecture became sculpture, molded into a work of art.

Once a fourteen-year-old boy wrote to Wright and asked him if he would please explain what an architect did. Wright answered:

Dear Mr. Philip,
My definition of Architect:
arch = chief or highest (i.e., archbishop, archetype = Master)
+ *tect* = technique, technology (i.e., the Know-How)
= Architect: *Master of the Know-How!*
Sincerely,
Frank Lloyd Wright

Wright has been called the father of modern architecture. Architects of the international style, such as Walter Gropius, Ludwig Mies van der Rohe, and Philip Johnson, who made sleek boxlike structures of steel and glass, acknowledged Wright's importance and his influence on their work.

In 1949, Philip Johnson wrote, "In my opinion, Frank Lloyd Wright is the greatest living architect, and for many reasons. He is the founder of modern architecture as we know it in the West, the originator of so many styles that his emulators are invariably a decade or so behind. . . . There can be no disagreement . . . that he is the most influential architect of our century."

Critics have labeled Wright arrogant, vain, egotistical, eccentric, outspoken, stubborn, and contradictory. He believed he was the greatest architect of all time. One day while he was working at his drafting table, one of his apprentices overheard him muttering to himself, "I am a genius." Indeed, Wright was a rebel and a nonconformist all his life and was proud of it. He wore his hair long, carried a cane, and designed his own unusual suits and capes. His personal and professional life gained him notoriety as well as fame.

But the very traits that he was criticized for may have enabled him to continue working in the face of setbacks and sorrows that would have destroyed a less confident person. Scholars continue to analyze Wright's work. New books and articles about him are published every year. Museums throughout the world exhibit his art. Why all this fuss about someone who died so long ago? Why is Wright great?

I Was Born

BEFORE FRANK LLOYD WRIGHT was born, his mother, Anna Lloyd Jones, decided he would be an architect. Even while she was pregnant, she hung engravings of English cathedrals in her future child's room to influence him right from the start. She was convinced her baby would be a boy and that he would build beautiful buildings.

Chapter Two

"I was born an architect," Wright boasted.

On June 8, 1867, he was born in Richland Center in southern Wisconsin. For years controversy surrounded his birth date. As an adult, Wright maintained he was born in 1869. He liked creating myths about himself, and when he wrote his autobiography, he altered many details of his life.

An Architect

(Previous page) **THE EXTERIOR OF THE JOHN STORER HOUSE IN HOLLYWOOD, CALIFORNIA.**

(Above) **FRANK LLOYD WRIGHT TOOK THIS PICTURE OF THE WOMEN WHO STRONGLY INFLUENCED HIS CAREER: TO THE LEFT, HIS MOTHER, ANNA LLOYD JONES, AND HER TWO SISTERS—AUNT NELL IN THE CHAIR AND AUNT JANE SEATED ON THE GROUND.**

His mother, Anna Lloyd Jones, descended from Welsh pioneers who settled in a valley by the Wisconsin River because it reminded them of south Wales. They lovingly called their new home "The Valley." Four of Anna's brothers took up farming there, and she and her sisters taught school. Wright adored his aunts and uncles and wanted to look like them—tall, dark, and handsome. Instead he resembled his father, William Russel Cary Wright, who was short and had delicate features. William Wright grew up in New England and in his youth attended college, which was unusual at the time. Multitalented, he studied law and medicine, then became superintendent of schools in Wisconsin, and later became a minister, but his real love was music. He earned a living by traveling around the country giving music lessons and may have met Anna at a songfest or through their work in education. They were married on August 17, 1866, but were unhappy almost from the start.

The family moved often as William tried one job and then another in his search

18

for success and self-fulfillment. These frequent moves and the ensuing tension between his parents may have driven Wright to yearn for a perfect, permanent home—a warm, sheltering place offering the peace he didn't experience as a child.

When Wright was two, his sister, Mary Jane, nicknamed Jennie, was born. His other sister, Margaret Ellen, known as Maginel, was born a few years later in Weymouth, Massachusetts. Wright attended private school in Weymouth but his real learning took place at home.

Anna bought an educational toy called "Froebel Gifts for art building" for her son that proved to be one of the greatest influences on his approach to architecture. It was created by a German educator named Friedrich Froebel, who invented the concept of the kindergarten. Froebel believed young children could learn with their imaginations through guided play. The Gifts consisted of twenty sets, beginning with yarn balls of wool and wooden blocks, triangles, and cylinders. Children received one set at a time with instructions and built structures on a grid. The rules helped children see geometric forms in nature and understand the principles of good design.

Every night after supper Wright and his sister Jennie would sit at a low mahogany table with their mother and

WILLIAM RUSSEL CARY WRIGHT PASSIONATELY LOVED MUSIC AND TAUGHT HIS SON, FRANK, HOW TO PLAY THE PIANO AND HOW TO COMPOSE.

play with the Froebel "toys" for hours. When Wright was in his seventies, he clearly remembered this pleasure. "Eventually I was to construct designs in other mediums," he said, "but the smooth cardboard triangles and maplewood blocks were most important. All are in my fingers to this day. . . . Design was recreation!"

Wright also loved to draw with colored pencils and crayons. At one point his mother scraped enough money together for oil painting lessons because she

THESE FROEBEL BLOCKS AND OTHER "GIFTS" ARE LIKE THE
ONES WRIGHT PLAYED WITH AS A CHILD. NOTICE THE SIMILARITY
BETWEEN THE WOODEN BLOCKS AND THE CEMENT BLOCKS
WRIGHT USED TO BUILD THE STORER HOUSE.

thought it would help him become an architect. What really helped him, though, was his mother's teaching à la Froebel. On long walks together they picked wildflowers and leaves, and Anna pointed out their geometric designs and intricate patterns and colors.

From his father Wright received a different kind of training. He learned how to design through music. William taught his son "to see a great symphony as an *edifice of sound*." Both a symphony and a house needed structure or form; their parts had to be arranged in a certain order. Both required mathematics. Wright began to "listen to music as a kind of building." He realized that architecture and music involved the same creative process of going from the general to the particular theme and variations. To create harmony in a house, he related the parts to the whole, just as in a symphony the movements relate to the main theme.

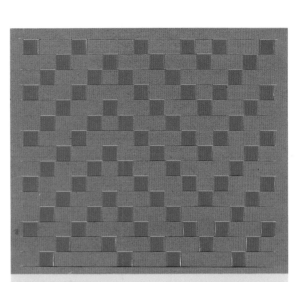

WRIGHT SAVED THIS PAPER WEAVING EXERCISE FROM HIS OWN SET OF FROEBEL'S GIFTS. THE COLORS AND DESIGN INSPIRED HIS APPROACH TO HIS ADULT WORK.

Wright developed a lifelong love of music from his father. When he was an adult he always hummed at the drafting table and listened to recordings of music by Bach and Beethoven while he worked. Every house he lived in had a piano.

Wright admired his talented father and shared his pleasure in solo activities. He preferred reading, drawing, and listening to music over playing with other boys. Above all, Wright liked to daydream. His mother worried that he was

**FRANK LLOYD WRIGHT AT
THE AGE OF EIGHT OR NINE.**

spending too much time alone. In 1878 the family moved back to Spring Green, Wisconsin, when Wright was around eleven, and Anna sent him to work on his Uncle James's farm in The Valley. The experience affected him deeply and shaped him as an artist.

At first Wright hated the farm. Most of all, he hated his chores. His worst job was taking care of the cows. He fed them, milked them, took them out to pasture, and brought them home again. His day began at 4:00 A.M. and then at night, after supper, Wright would fall into bed, exhausted. Now he understood the meaning of the Lloyd Jones family motto: "Add 'tired' to 'tired' and add it again—and add it yet again."

A few times Wright ran away but his uncles found him and brought him back. Uncle Enos said, "Work is an adventure that makes strong men and finishes weak ones," and Wright never forgot that advice. After a while he became used to farming. His muscles developed and so did his self-confidence.

For five years in a row, Wright spent his summers on the family's farm. In the winters he went to public school in Madison. Looking back he regarded this period of his life as a good influence. So good that when he was much older and formed a Fellowship for aspiring architects, he insisted his apprentices spend a few hours each day working on a farm. The experience, he thought, would teach them what real effort and achievement were all about.

While young Wright toughed out his farm days, he discovered the wonder and beauty of nature. On Sundays he gathered pine boughs and wildflowers to decorate the pulpit in the family chapel. Colors on the Wisconsin farm thrilled him. "Night shadows so wonderfully blue, white birches gleaming," the tall red lilies growing in the meadow-grass. Later when he became an architect, he remembered the lily and transformed it into a red square for his signature crest.

Wright even loved weeds, and as a young architect he would gather them on the prairie and arrange them in copper urns and vases he had designed himself. He photographed them and printed some of the pictures in a book called *The House Beautiful*. To decorate the book he drew pen-and-ink weed borders.

As a boy on the farm, Wright observed everything around him. "Everything has its plan," he would say. He saw that the shapes of natural things, like trees and flowers, were determined by their function. Parts related harmoniously to the whole. The petals of a flower, the branches of a tree were "natural to that thing." The trees were like different kinds of buildings.

WRIGHT PHOTOGRAPHED THIS WILDFLOWER AND PRINTED THE IMAGE HIMSELF ON HANDMADE JAPANESE PAPER. HE HAD A DARKROOM OFF THE BALCONY OF HIS OAK PARK STUDIO.

Similarly, Wright wanted the shapes of all of his buildings to be determined by the purposes they served. "Form and function are one," he said. He was beginning to formulate his principles of organic architecture. Nature was so important to him, he spelled the word with a capital N in his writings as an adult.

Living creatures also interested Wright. He studied their "fascinating structure, color pattern, strange movements. . . ." These observations stayed with him and gave him ideas for work he was to construct later.

Twenty years later, in 1902, when Wright designed the Dana House in Springfield, Illinois, he created a butterfly motif for art glass windows and chandeliers. The patterns are characteristically geometric. Yet the motif in the entryway transom suggests the fluttering motion of real butterflies. The art glass connects the indoors with the outdoors. This is what Wright meant by organic architecture. He learned much more from nature than from school and said he remembered very little about his formal education. "A blank," he wrote, "except for colorful experiences that had nothing specific about them. Like dipping the gold braid hanging down the back of the pretty girl sitting in front, into the inkwell of my school desk and drawing with it."

WRIGHT DREW THIS INTRICATE BORDER FREEHAND, BASING HIS DESIGN ON PLANT FORMS. THE BORDERS FRAMED TEXT WRITTEN BY HIS FRIEND WILLIAM C. GANNET FOR *THE HOUSE BEAUTIFUL*.

WRIGHT'S CLIENT, SUSAN LAWRENCE DANA, WANTED
THE BUTTERFLY AS A MOTIF FOR HER HOUSE. WRIGHT OBLIGED
WITH THIS MAGNIFICENT ART GLASS TRANSOM
FOR THE ARCHED ENTRYWAY.

For Wright the most memorable thing that happened when he was twelve years old was meeting a crippled boy named Robie Lamp. They lived at the same end of town. One day Wright saw some bullies trying to bury Robie in a pile of autumn leaves. Wright, strong after his summer's work at the farm, rescued Robie and they became best friends.

The boys spent hours together drawing, printing cards on their secondhand press, and making kites and sleds. They both liked to invent things. Once they started to build a pedal-driven water boat called the "Frankenrob." They also loved to read.

Some of Wright's favorite books were John Ruskin's *The Seven Lamps of Architecture* (1849), a gift from his aunts, and the story of Aladdin in *The Arabian Nights*, which captured his imagination. He thought of himself as a kind of Aladdin with magical powers. Wright's heroes were Henry David Thoreau, Ralph Waldo Emerson, and Walt Whitman. From them he inherited a nineteenth-century view celebrating space, nature, and the individual. Wright embraced the message in Emerson's essay, "Self-Reliance": "There is a time in every man's education when he arrives at the conviction that envy is ignorance; that imitation is suicide; that he must take himself for better, for worse, as his portion. . . . Trust thyself. . . ."

Wright did trust himself, and he learned from his own experiences.

One day, during his high school years, as he was walking past the state capitol in Madison, he heard a roar and saw the new wing collapse in a cloud of lime dust. Some people were trapped inside. Others ran out bleeding and fell on the front lawn. The fire department arrived quickly and kept spectators back, but Wright stayed for hours, "too heart-sick to go away."

When Wright finally went home that night, he dreamt about the tragedy and couldn't get it out of his mind. Later he learned that the interior columns had collapsed because they were rotted at the core. The architect had made them unusually large and the contractor had filled them with rubble—broken bricks and stones—to keep expenses down. Still, the architect was held responsible for the tragedy and never built another building. Wright learned a valuable lesson about the importance of safe construction. When he began doing his own building in later years, he always used first-rate materials and looked after every detail.

Around the time of the accident, his parents' marriage ended in divorce. In April 1885, when Wright was seventeen, his father left. Wright sided with his mother, and he and his sisters stayed with her. They suffered terribly. Wright's own broken home may have driven him to create beautiful homes for other

American families.

In those days very few people divorced. Those who did were considered a disgrace. And if a minister got divorced, something was really wrong. Now there was a stigma on the Wrights, and neighbors in Madison didn't want their children to associate with them. Even Robie Lamp's parents didn't welcome Wright in their house anymore. In spite of that, Wright and Robie remained friends for life and both went to study at the University of Wisconsin.

Wright entered as a special student in engineering when he was eighteen. There are no records to show that he ever graduated from high school. He seems to have dropped out around the time his parents split up.

Other young people his age who wanted to become architects usually went to architecture school, such as the Massachusetts Institute of Technology (MIT), and enrolled in a four-year program. Some went on to the Ecole des Beaux-Arts (School of Fine Arts), Paris, to complete their training, but Wright couldn't afford this expensive education. He learned by doing. His mother helped arrange for him to work part time for Allan D. Conover, a professor of civil engineering at the university and a local builder.

As usual Wright didn't think much of school. Summing up the experience, he said, "Never learned anything. . . . About the only thing I gained from my university years was a corn from wearing toothpick shoes." Wright's shoes had extremely pointed toes and were all the rage for college boys at the time. Wright was a natty dresser and managed to look dapper even on a budget. Looking smart and dressing impeccably was to be a lifelong passion.

The most important part of his brief university training was his apprenticeship with Conover, who supervised the execution of buildings designed by others. Some of these buildings were on the university's campus, such as a new Science Hall.

One cold winter night, Wright went over to inspect progress at the new

Science Hall and discovered a flaw in the construction. Some plates that hold together portions or members of the trusses, the structural frame of the roof, were not secured. The trusses had been left hanging dangerously. Wright, concerned with safety, climbed the wooden ladder to the top of the truss supporting the roof. The rungs were slippery with ice but he went to the very top and stayed until he got the clips loose and dropped them down so they could be bolted properly the next day. He was beginning to feel an architect's responsibility to his building. Now he felt ready to start designing.

When he heard that his Uncle Jenkin Lloyd Jones planned to build a new chapel for the family in The Valley, Wright sent him some sketches showing his ideas for the project. However, his uncle gave the job to Joseph Lyman Silsbee, a Chicago architect. Wright was allowed to work on the interior design and it is said he patterned the ceiling in squares. He was also given the opportunity to publish a rendering of the chapel in the January 1887 issue of the *Annual* of All Souls Unitarian Church, Silsbee's other project for Jenkin. It was his first published architectural drawing.

Inasmuch as Wright had a taste of real experience, he wanted more. Today's architecture students study for four or five years and then work as apprentices for three more years before becoming eligible to take their license exams. But Wright felt ready to begin work after only two semesters at the university. Besides, he hated to see his mother and sisters making such sacrifices in order to send him to school.

When he told his mother he wanted to drop out and go to Chicago so he could "begin to be an architect right away," she was horrified. How could he think of leaving the university before the semester was over, much less before he graduated and earned his degree?

Wright pleaded his case: "There are great architects in Chicago, Mother, so there must be great buildings too. I am going to be an architect. You want me to be one. I am nowhere near it here." He threatened to go without her approval. Finally he persuaded his mother to write a letter to her brother, Jenkin, who was building a church for his congregation in Chicago. Maybe he could help Wright find work.

WRIGHT WAS ABOUT NINETEEN WHEN THIS PICTURE WAS TAKEN. HE WROTE THE CAPTION: "THE REBELLIOUS STUDENT SHORTLY AFTER ARRIVING IN CHICAGO."

Anna sent the letter. Jenkin's answer read: "On no account let the young man come to Chicago. He should stay in Madison and finish his education. . . . If he came here he would only waste himself on fine clothes and girls."

But Wright immediately sold a few things, secretly bought a train ticket to Chicago, and kept the change for food and a hotel. On a February afternoon in 1887 when he was nineteen years old, Wright hopped on the Northwestern train bound for Chicago. A couple of friends went with him. One was a young farmhand, the other a student at his aunts' Hillside Home School back in Spring Green. The student conveniently happened to be the son of a Chicago millionaire.

Wright had learned two valuable lessons from the university: the importance of safe construction and of hard work.

29

The Young Man

YOUNG MR. WRIGHT, ON his own for the first time, arrived in Chicago on a rainy night. The next day he started to look for work and within a week was hired by Joseph Silsbee, the architect who had designed Unity Chapel for Wright's family and All Souls Unitarian Church for Uncle Jenkin.

Chapter Three

On his first day in the office, Wright struck up a friendship with another young draftsman, Cecil Corwin. The two discovered they had much in common—both were sons of ministers and loved music as well as architecture. Cecil treated Wright to lunch and invited him to stay at his house. That night Wright borrowed $10 from him to send to his mother

In Architecture

(Previous page) THE HILLSIDE HOME SCHOOL WAS WRIGHT'S FIRST BUILDING. HIS CLIENTS WERE HIS AUNTS NELL AND JANE, WHO FOUNDED THE COEDUCATIONAL BOARDING SCHOOL. IN LATER YEARS, WRIGHT ADOPTED THEIR EDUCATIONAL CREDO OF LEARNING BY DOING.

(Left) CATHERINE TOBIN WRIGHT IS WEARING A DRESS DESIGNED BY HER HUSBAND, FRANK LLOYD WRIGHT. HE PROBABLY TOOK THE PICTURE, TOO.

and promised to pay it back. Borrowing money and getting into debt proved to be one of Wright's bad habits for life.

During the following months, Wright enjoyed working for Silsbee and learned much from him. Silsbee was a popular architect of the American Shingle Style. Shingle Style houses were characteristically asymmetrical. Viewed from the front, the two sides were not the same. This lack of symmetry created an informal, picturesque effect. The houses were an elaborate combination of oversized triangular gable roofs, big porches, protruding balconies, bay windows, and tall chimneys. Wood shingles covered every exterior surface and unified the design.

In Silsbee's office, Wright and the other draftsmen developed floor plans from the architect's freehand sketches. Then Silsbee corrected the working drawings. Silsbee recognized Wright's talent and let him take on extra jobs to gain recognition.

One freelance project was a school building in Wisconsin for his aunts Nell and Jane. In 1886 his aunts had established Hillside Home School on the family's farmland. There, boys and girls farmed, cooked, sewed, played golf, and went on nature walks in addition to studying academic subjects. Aunt Nell asked Wright to submit sketches for a new building and hired him as the architect. Wright's design derived from the Shingle Style. The school building was covered with wood shingles and had a big arched front porch and large triangular gables. This was Wright's first commission and he was pleased with the way his career was progressing. But his mother missed him terribly.

In those days, before the telephone was a common household item, they kept in touch by writing. A letter of Anna's began, "My dear Frank, It is two weeks since I wrote to you but I think of you every day." Further on she mentioned his problem budgeting money. She knew his tendency to be extravagant. Her son was a clotheshorse. Evidently, he had left Madison without settling a debt for cloth dancing shoes.

Wright's mother gave him advice about his career and told him to stick with his job. But Wright was ambitious and eager to move ahead. After three months with Silsbee he asked for a raise and got it. However, when he asked for a second raise and didn't get it, he quit. He quickly found another job, but the architects there expected him to design houses. Since Wright didn't know how to yet, he went back to Silsbee, who rehired him.

In her letters, Anna again urged Wright to stay. She also told him how to conduct himself with young ladies. "Don't regard girls as playthings," she wrote. . . ."I hope you will find companionship in Uncle Jenk's church."

Uncle Jenkin's All Souls Church was Unitarian and offered a friendly atmosphere with many social activities. Wright attended a study club there. At the end of the class there was a costume party and everyone dressed up as characters from Victor Hugo's *Les Misérables*. Wright went as a dashing French officer. During a break for refreshments, a pretty girl in pink came rushing across the dance floor and collided with him. She fell down and Wright helped her up. Although she laughed it off and said it was her fault, he politely led her over to her parents to apologize.

They were Mr. and Mrs. Tobin, a prosperous south-side couple. Their daughter was Catherine, nicknamed Kitty. She was sixteen and in high school. The Tobins invited Wright to Sunday dinner the next day and that marked the beginning of a friendship that blossomed into a romance.

Even though the Tobins approved, Wright's mother did not. Anna was very possessive of her son and resented his growing attachment to Kitty. Anna had heard about the relationship from her brother Jenkin and found out more when she sold her house and moved to Chicago. Wright felt responsible for his mother and sent for her and his sister Maginel. His other sister Jennie stayed in Wisconsin. She was teaching piano and singing at Hillside Home School and moved to Chicago later on. Wright wanted them all to live on the North Shore but Anna worried about the strong winds off the lake and chose Oak Park instead.

Oak Park was a lovely suburb, like a village on the outskirts of Chicago. Big trees shaded the streets. Bankers, stockbrokers, and department store owners lived there and commuted to their downtown offices. Houses were built there in the Queen Anne and Shingle styles.

Queen Anne houses were asymmetrical, too, and featured pointed roofs, corner hexagonal towers, and wraparound porches. In general, their outside surfaces were covered in clapboard (a long, thin wood board) and a variety of patterned shingles. The inside walls were covered with flowery Victorian wallpaper. Dark rooms were crammed with ornately carved furniture. Some people thought these houses were charming. To Wright they looked silly and uncomfortable.

At first Wright and his mother and Maginel rented rooms in Oak Park. He worked hard at Silsbee's office and learned his craft. At the same time he was developing his own ideas about architecture and discussed them with Cecil, who thought Silsbee was right in giving people the kind of houses they wanted. Wright argued that an architect should design "the best he knew how to do. Not as he was *told* to do it, but as he *saw* it for himself." Cecil said to Wright, "Whom are you going to build homes for?" But Wright wanted to be an architect who served his clients and respected their needs and wishes, while making an artistic statement of his own. In his search for a personal form of expression, he intuitively knew it was time to leave Silsbee.

Chicago architecture, at the turn of the century, was the most daring and

THE EXTERIOR OF WRIGHT'S OAK PARK HOME IS SHOWN AS IT LOOKED IN 1890, WITH CATHERINE STANDING IN THE DOORWAY. THE OVERSIZED TRIANGULAR GABLE IS AN ENLARGED SIMPLIFIED VERSION OF THE ONE ON THE HILLSIDE HOME SCHOOL BUILDING.

forward-looking in the country. One of the leading firms in the city was headed by two men—Dankmar Adler and Louis Sullivan. Adler was an engineer who specialized in acoustics, lighting, and ventilation. Sullivan was a brilliant young architect. At thirty-one, Wright was on the threshold of his fame and was to design skyscrapers as no one else could do, balancing their height with delicate ornamentation.

Sullivan had been trained at MIT and at the Beaux-Arts and was already a leading figure in the movement later known as the Chicago School of Architecture. His intricate organic patterns were inspired by nature. Like Wright he believed that good designers must be "good observers first, then good draftsmen."

Wright had long admired Adler and Sullivan's work, and when he heard that they were looking for an outstanding draftsman, he raced over for an interview. Sullivan hired him on the merit of his drawings. Wright was twenty years old. His new job was to transform Sullivan's sketches for the interior of an auditorium he was building into working drawings to be used for construction.

Wright stayed with Sullivan for nearly seven years. In his own words, he became "a good pencil in the master's hand," affectionately referring to his boss as *Lieber Meister* (beloved master). Wright rapidly rose to the top of the large firm and was given a private office adjoining Sullivan's. Soon he became head of the Planning and Designing Department and supervised thirty other draftsmen. Naturally they were jealous of Wright and picked fights with him. According to Wright, he secretly took boxing lessons to prepare for a match with one of the "Adler & Sullivan" gang. Another time he defended himself with his T square.

Wright and Sullivan formed a close friendship. Both men were great artists, philosophers, and lovers of poetry and music. They spent hours talking. Some architectural historians say that Sullivan learned as much from Wright as the apprentice did from his master.

After Wright had worked at Adler & Sullivan for about a year, he wanted to marry Kitty, the pretty girl he had fallen for at the costume party. Anna strongly objected. She thought her son and Kitty were much too young to get married.

Eventually Anna came around and lent him money from the sale of her house in Madison to buy a large piece of property with a house on one part of it. They lived there while Wright designed another house on his part of the land for his bride-to-be. He asked Sullivan for financial help and the firm gave him a five-year contract and loaned him money. Wright took Sullivan to Oak Park to see the wooded corner lot. It was on the best street in town, and it was planted with lilacs, violets, and lilies of the valley.

Wright married Kitty on June 1, 1889. She was eighteen and he was almost twenty-two. They lived with Anna and Maginel while their own house was under construction and moved into it just before their first baby was born the following spring.

According to Maginel, Wright's house was "charming and original. It was greatly admired in the neighborhood. . . ." It has also been said that Wright modeled the house upon the published designs of two shingled houses by another architect. Certainly the house shows traits of the Shingle Style. Wright had received good training from Silsbee and his influence appeared in Wright's work. However, Wright was moving away from the picturesque toward simpler forms and symmetrical designs.

Wright's house reflects his personal touch in the low sheltering roof and the large terrace at the front connecting the house to the earth. Stone urns at the entrance hold flowers. When the urns are viewed from above, below, or the side, they reveal a three-dimensional representation of Wright's early logo or symbol: a cross within a circle within a square.

Inside, the house centers around a fireplace. Inglenook seats in a cozy corner near the hearth emphasize family togetherness. Above the inglenook seats there are wood-trimmed openings that look like panels in the wall. Over the mantel a false opening is actually a mirror. These were some of Wright's tricks to make small spaces appear larger.

When his daughters were teenagers, they used to sit along the fireplace with their boyfriends, one couple on each side, and hold hands. Their younger brothers would sneak up and shoot wads of paper at them through the openings to the library and dining room.

Wright designed his own dining room table and high-backed chairs with a matching high chair to create a room within a room. These pieces were Wright's first experiment in freestanding furniture and were made for him by craftsmen. Throughout his career, Wright depended on many talented craftspeople to execute his designs. Although it was expensive to have pieces custom-made, Wright couldn't find simple, well-constructed furniture suited to his architecture, so he designed his own.

Over the dining room table, an electric light filters through a ceiling grille carved in an abstract pattern of branches and leaves. This was probably the first use of recessed indirect lighting. Natural light in the room comes through art glass windows designed by Wright in a stylized lotus pattern. Art glass is like stained glass: pieces of colored or clear glass are assembled and held together by metal bars. The windows in the dining room added charm and also gave the family privacy. The Wrights could look out while they were eating but their neighbors couldn't see in.

For a few years Wright used the large front room on the second floor as a studio. Then, as his family grew, he changed and expanded the house. Change was his guiding principle.

In 1890, his son Lloyd was born. Then came John, Catherine, David, Frances, and Robert Llewellyn. Wright turned the large room into a bedroom for his six children and divided it with a low partition. Girls slept on one side, boys on the

WARM EARTH TONES CHARACTERIZE THE DINING ROOM IN
FRANK LLOYD WRIGHT'S HOME. RED CLAY TILES COVER THE FLOOR
AND HEARTH. THE TILED FIREPLACE IS LOCATED AT ONE END OF THE
ROOM, FACING THE ART GLASS BAY WINDOWS.

other. When Catherine and Frances had slumber parties, their brothers threw pillows across the wall.

Wright created a magnificent playroom for them. Its barrel-vaulted ceiling is eighteen feet high. During the winter when the children had to play indoors, the room was large enough to serve as a gymnasium. Above a huge fireplace at one end there is a mural painted by Orlando Giannini, depicting a scene from *The Arabian Nights*. At the other end there is a gallery or raised balcony. The children used to put on plays for their neighborhood friends and charged admission for gallery seats. A grand piano was placed into the wall under the gallery steps and suspended by an iron strap. Wright didn't like the look of the piano, so only the keyboard shows. He organized a family orchestra and assigned each child an instrument.

WRIGHT'S CHILDREN POSE ON THE VERANDA OF THEIR HOUSE. FROM FAR LEFT: FRANCES, LLOYD, DAVID, LLEWELLYN, CATHERINE, AND JOHN.

Every Christmas an enormous tree stood in the center of the playroom. Lit candles were attached to the branches and a bucket of water was placed nearby in case of fire. On Christmas morning the children stood in the bedroom corridors, waiting for their father to get up so they could go into the playroom and open their presents.

Wright wanted them to grow up in a beautiful environment. The art glass windows in the playroom and a carved grille covering the skylight have patterns of stylized leaves. His daughter Catherine recalled, ". . . the ceiling was vaulted with one of the most beautiful pieces of scrollwork I have ever seen." And John remembered, "My first impression upon coming into the playroom from the narrow, long, low-arched, dimly lighted passageway that led to it was its great height and brilliant light. . . ." Wright repeatedly used this device of changing ceiling height from very low to very high to make spaces exciting and seem larger than they actually were.

Young Catherine was upset that their house was so different from everyone else's. Once she painted her wooden walls with white enamel and replaced her simple window hangings with frilly dotted Swiss curtains so that her room would look like her friend's across the street. But what she disliked most was the tree in the kitchen.

The tree came to be there when Wright added a studio and connected it to the main house with a passageway. A willow tree stood in the way, and rather than cut it down, he allowed it to grow through the roof. People came by to see it and called it "the house with the tree through the roof." Wright even set the icebox between the arms of the tree. Whenever it rained there were puddles everywhere and Catherine and her mother had to mop them up.

Wright left the job of raising the children to his wife, and he devoted himself to his architecture. When Wright first moved into his house he still worked for Adler & Sullivan. Since they were interested in commercial projects, they turned commissions for houses over to him. Wright designed a summer house for Sullivan in Ocean Springs, Mississippi. At the same time, he supervised drawings for the Schiller Building and other Chicago skyscrapers designed by Sullivan. Even so, Wright wasn't earning enough money to pay his bills.

Wright loved beautiful things and couldn't do without them—books, Oriental rugs, and original artwork. He wanted his handsome children to wear "swell duds" like his, and took them downtown shopping once a year. Wright said, "So long as we had the luxuries, the necessities could pretty well take care

of themselves." But that wasn't true. The grocer and the butcher had to be paid.

Secretly Wright began moonlighting. He took on extra jobs after he finished his regular work in the Adler & Sullivan office. At night in his studio he designed houses for clients who privately commissioned him. Wright called these commissions his "bootlegged" houses. When Sullivan found out about them he was furious. Wright argued that his nighttime work didn't interfere with his daytime performance for the firm, but in later years he realized he was wrong. After a blowup, Wright left and didn't see Sullivan again for twelve years.

Now Wright was truly out on his own.

THE PLAYROOM LOOKING EAST, SHOWING THE BARREL VAULT, CARVED CEILING GRILLE, FIREPLACE, WINDOW SEATS, AND BUILT-IN CUPBOARDS, WHERE THE CHILDREN KEPT THEIR TOYS.

A Natural

IN 1893, WHEN WRIGHT was twenty-six, he opened an office with Cecil Corwin, the good friend he had met at Silsbee's. Now Wright had a chance to build a more "natural" house.

Fashionable houses of the period reflected foreign styles. Architects combined a hodgepodge of domes, corner towers, rosette ornaments, bay

Chapter Four

windows, fancy porches, and Greek columns to suit the whims of their clients. The richer the client, the taller and bigger the house. Interiors consisted of "boxes beside or inside other boxes called *rooms*."

Wright wanted to build from the inside out. What kind of spaces, he wondered, would best suit the needs of an American family? What kind

House

of house would preserve family life and make it better? How could machinery and materials be used properly?

His first client was William H. Winslow, who commissioned Wright to design a house and stables at River Forest, a suburb west of Oak Park. The symmetrical façade or front of the house looks modern in its stark simplicity. The

well-placed front door and the plain brick walls, devoid of fussy trim and ornamentation, are innovations. So is the garage floor with a turntable to turn the car around.

Wright said that the significance of the house was its sense of shelter created by a broad overhang. The roof extends about six feet beyond the walls. The main

house and stables are considered a masterpiece because of their simplicity, originality, and graceful proportions. Many people came to see it. Some ridiculed it. But others loved it.

Louis Sullivan saw the house and commented to Winslow that it demonstrated Wright's individuality. Daniel Burnham, another well-known Chicago architect, and Ed Waller, a wealthy neighbor of Winslow's, made Wright a generous offer. They proposed to send him to the Beaux-Arts in Paris for four years, all expenses paid, if he would design classical houses upon his return. Wright refused. The men were dumbfounded.

Wright explained that he wanted to keep his own individual ideas. In his opinion Beaux-Arts training produced cookie-cutter architects who copied old European styles unsuited to the American landscape and culture.

Burnham said that the success of the World's Columbian Exposition in Chicago that year, 1893, indicated the great influence Classical architecture was going to have on America. Wright thought the only good things from that Exposition were Louis Sullivan's Transportation Building and the exhibit from Japan.

The long Transportation Building, ornamented on the outside with intricate patterns, featured the Golden Doorway, an entrance consisting of five concentric arches set within a single grand arch. Wright liked the contrast of the strong horizontal line of the building with the semicircles in the entryway.

The Japanese exhibit was a replica of a wooden temple. It had an ample roof with upturned eaves. In place of solid walls there were sliding screens that allowed daylight and fresh air to enter continuously. On display in the temple was a collection of Japanese seventeenth- and eighteenth-century prints, but Wright was already familiar with these. His former employer, Silsbee, collected Oriental art.

After the Winslow house, Wright designed an English Tudor half-timbered house for Nathan Moore because Moore said, "he didn't want anything like that Winslow house so that he would have to go around back ways to the train to avoid being laughed at. . . ." Wright took the job because he needed the money to support his family. Yet he continued to search for a more personalized architecture. "Ideas had naturally begun to come to me," he wrote, "as to a more natural house. Each house I built I longed for the chance to build another."

His next commission, however, was for a windmill. In 1897, his aunts asked him to build a new water tower for the Hillside Home School in Wisconsin. Wright's unusual design was his first blending of architecture and engineering. He invented his taproot principle and rooted the tower like a tree so it wouldn't fall. It was anchored deep in a stone foundation and secured with metal straps. Wright called his structure "Romeo and Juliet" because the interlocking forms suggest the Shakespearean lovers. "Romeo," he said, "will do all the work and Juliet cuddle alongside to support and exalt him."

Around this time Wright's friend Cecil gave up architecture and left Chicago. Wright moved his practice to the Steinway Hall, where other bright young architects had their offices, and in 1898 he built the studio next to his house. Wright was so busy that his children didn't see much of him except at mealtime. Sometimes they sneaked out to the balcony overlooking the drafting room and

ALTHOUGH WRIGHT DENIED ANY DIRECT INFLUENCE FROM JAPANESE
ARCHITECTURE, THE SLIGHTLY UPTURNED EAVES (EDGES OF THE ROOF)
OF THE DANA HOUSE RESEMBLE THOSE OF THE PAGODAS IN THE
JAPANESE PRINTS THAT WRIGHT STUDIED.

peeked at him going over plans with a client. Or they "quietly" threw things down on the heads of the draftsmen.

As Wright's practice grew, he hired more men and women to assist him. They adored him and dressed the way he did, with flowing ties and smocks. Some of them had been associated with Wright at Steinway Hall. Wright and his contemporaries were developing a new kind of house design and the movement was called the Prairie School. It echoed the spirit and look of the American Midwest. The emphasis was on simplicity and a respect for materials. With the help of his staff during the next decade, Wright built at least eighty-one Prairie Houses and planned forty-nine more. Some were as far away as Buffalo, New York, and Montecito, California. Then how could they be called Prairie Houses?

All of them expressed shelter, security, and privacy with their horizontal lines, low-spreading roofs, and concealed entrances. For every house, Wright used local materials and used the materials naturally. Brick looked like brick, wood showed its color and grain. He related each house to its natural setting as if it had grown out of the ground.

On the prairie, Wright designed houses low and parallel to the earth. He coined the word "streamlined" to describe this characteristic. He did away with high stuffy attics and damp cellars. Wright wanted to reduce the number of parts of a house to a minimum. He thought of the house as essentially one free-flowing space centered around a fireplace. There were no walled partitions except for private areas, such as bedrooms, kitchens, and bathrooms. Indoor plumbing had just come in, around 1890, along with electricity and steam heat.

THE SUMAC WINDOW IN THE DANA HOUSE ALLOWS LIGHT TO COME IN, BUT THE COLORFUL PATTERN ALSO SERVES AS A SCREEN TO ENSURE PRIVACY.

Wright dramatically lowered and sloped ceilings to make rooms easier to heat, cool, and light and to create intimacy. The typical ceiling in a Victorian house was eleven or twelve feet high. Wright brought the scale down to fit a human being—himself. "It has been said," he wrote, "that were I three inches taller than 5'8½", all my houses would have been quite different in proportion." He also lowered and enlarged windows to connect the indoors with the outdoors.

Some of the Prairie Houses were small, such as Wright's drawing of a model house, *A Home in a Prairie Town*, published in the *Ladies' Home Journal* in February 1901. In July, the magazine published a second drawing called *A Small House with 'Lots of Room in It.'*

Other Prairie Houses were large. One of the most elaborate is the Dana House in Springfield, Illinois, with thirty-five rooms. Susan Lawrence Dana was a wealthy widow who hired Wright to design a mansion suitable for entertaining lavishly. She gave Wright unlimited funds and the opportunity to show off his skills.

Planning and construction of the Dana House began in 1902, and the magnificent house was completed in 1904. It rises gracefully from a corner city lot. The arched brick entryway is reminiscent of the Golden Doorway in Sullivan's Transportation Building. Architectural historians say this dramatic entrance suggests the opening of a cave.

Wright used thin, narrow buff-colored Roman bricks on the inside of the house as well as on the outside. Using the same material inside and out had never been done before. A stairway leads from the vestibule to a main hall, two stories high. Both the dining room and the studio gallery are barrel-vaulted like the playroom Wright created for his children. The main theme of the exquisite art glass doors and windows is the sumac, one of Wright's favorite shrubs that grows on the prairie. He created hundreds of geometric interpretations of the sumac. The prairie also gave Wright the colors for the house. On the train ride between Chicago and Springfield, he saw the soft green, mauve, gold, and rich russet-brown he used for the interior.

The same year the Dana House was completed, Wright designed a compact

one-story house in Oak Park for Edwin and Mamah Borthwick Cheney. The house was particularly significant because it sparked a relationship between Wright and Mrs. Cheney. She was a lovely, intelligent woman. Even though they were both already married, they felt attracted to each other.

Meanwhile, Wright kept busy. Although he was mainly considered a residential architect, he designed two public buildings during his Oak Park period that became landmarks: the Larkin Company Administration Building in Buffalo, New York, in 1904, and Unity Temple in Oak Park, Illinois, in 1905.

Since the site of the Larkin Building was located in a factory district near a railroad yard, Wright shut out the noise and dirt and focused on the interior. He created a simple, geometric brick building and pushed the staircases out to the four corners to form an open central courtyard inside. Natural light poured in through a skylight and in from bands of high windows on every floor or gallery. The top story had a restaurant and a conservatory with flowers and plants.

Eighteen hundred people worked together in open spaces on the main floor and on the upper galleries as they handled mail orders for Larkin soap. The top executives sat in the very center of the main floor, an unusual arrangement that gave them no privacy or status. But they were progressive. The Larkin Building was the first air-conditioned office building in America. Wright cleaned and cooled the air by using a combination of an air-purifying and cooling apparatus with a refrigeration machine.

The Larkin Building was also one of the first fireproofed buildings. Wright accomplished this by using a steel frame and bricks inside and out. He also designed for the building metal office furniture—another first—as an additional fireproofing measure. "I was a real Leonardo da Vinci when I built that building," Wright said. "Everything in it was my invention." As usual Wright favored art over comfort. A three-legged office chair he designed was so shaky that employees named it the "suicide chair." But Wright's favorite invention was the wall-hung toilet (designed to make mopping easier) and, along with it, the ceiling-hung stall partition.

Many European architects visited the Larkin Building and were greatly influ-

(*Opposite*) **A VIEW OF THE INTERIOR OF THE LARKIN BUILDING FROM THE BALCONY ACROSS THE COURTYARD. THE BALCONIES WERE INSCRIBED WITH INSPIRING WORDS: ENTHUSIASM. INTELLIGENCE. COOPERATION. ACTION. WRIGHT CONSIDERED THIS ONE OF HIS MOST IMPORTANT BUILDINGS.**

(*Left*) **WRIGHT DESIGNED STEEL ARMCHAIRS WITH LEATHER-COVERED SEATS FOR THE LARKIN BUILDING.**

THE MASSIVE GEOMETRIC SHAPES OF UNITY TEMPLE BEAR A RESEMBLANCE
TO A STRUCTURE MADE WITH FROEBEL'S WOODEN BLOCKS.

enced by Wright's design, a total integration of form and function. Ludwig Mies van der Rohe, a German-born architect, said, "Certainly I was very much impressed . . . by the office building in Buffalo. Who wouldn't be impressed?" Mies Van der Rohe's spare Lake Shore Drive apartment houses in Chicago bear a distinct resemblance to Wright's Larkin Building, and his Bacardi Office Building in Mexico features a large open room as a work space.

However, one critic who favored a more classical style thought the Larkin Building was "extremely ugly."

Nevertheless, more commissions poured into Wright's office. In February 1905, he took a break from his exhausting schedule and went on a vacation with friends who were also clients. Perhaps they knew about Wright's interest in Mrs. Cheney and wanted to distract him. At any rate, they invited Wright and his wife, Kitty, to go to Japan with them.

THE INTERIOR OF UNITY TEMPLE IS AMAZINGLY BRIGHT AND INTIMATE. LIGHT POURS IN THROUGH SKYLIGHTS AND HIGH BANDS OF WINDOWS. WHEN MEMBERS OF THE CONGREGATION EXIT, THEY WALK TOWARD THE PULPIT RATHER THAN AWAY FROM IT.

When Wright sailed into Yokohama Bay he was thrilled to discover that Japan looked "just like the prints" in his collection. During the trip Wright bought more prints and other pieces of art. The Japanese print reinforced the lesson of simplicity—"the elimination of the insignificant." He marveled at Japanese houses. "At last I had found one country on earth where simplicity, as natural, is supreme," he said.

Refreshed and inspired, Wright returned to Oak Park to receive an important commission. In June 1905, the old Unitarian Church burned down and a committee hired Wright to build a new one. They wanted a traditional New England church complete with a steeple. But Wright's idea was to create "a modern meeting-house and good-time place . . . a nobly simple room," scaled down to human proportions. "A *natural* building for natural Man."

With a budget of $45,000, Wright had to do something "cheap and direct." He chose concrete as a building material. The forms used to cast concrete were made of wood, so another way to cut costs was to cast one half then reuse the mold for the other side that was essentially identical. Thus he arrived at the cube, the motif for Unity Temple.

For weeks Wright developed the drawings and plans until he was ready to make a presentation to the committee. As soon as he received approval he proceeded to make a plaster model; he was then given a go-ahead and construction began. The powerful building with its massive shapes, piers, and roof slab looks like an abstract design made with Froebel blocks, the building toy Wright's mother had given him when he was a child. All the elements of Unity Temple are formed by straight lines. Wright demonstrated his genius by using squares and cubes over and over again without becoming monotonous. The interior space of the building defined its outer shape. Unity Temple was completed in 1907 and Wright was pleased.

THE LIVING ROOM OF THE COONLEY HOUSE. WRIGHT REPEATED
THE GEOMETRIC DESIGN TO CREATE AN INTERIOR THAT WAS QUIET,
UNCLUTTERED, AND COMFORTABLE.

"I knew I had the beginning of a great thing," he said, "a great truth in architecture."

Around this time Avery and Queene Coonley asked him to build a house for them and Wright considered it one of his most successful of this period. The large house is spread out over a spacious site. Wright planned it in wings or zones: the bedrooms in one wing, the living room in another, and so on. Once again he was allowed to design every detail—from the furniture, carpets, drapes, lamps, and exterior ceramic tile, down to table linens. It is said that he even designed dresses for Queene Coonley so that she would harmonize with her rooms. The estate with its lovely reflecting pool was one of Wright's most complete creations. Each part related to the whole and repeated the same geometric motif.

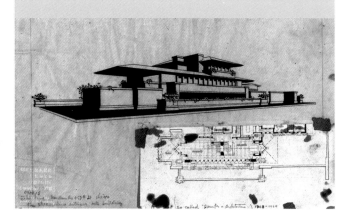

THE PRESENTATION INK DRAWING OF THE ROBIE HOUSE, PUBLISHED IN THE *WASMUTH PORTFOLIO*, ILLUSTRATES ITS LONG, LOW LINES. MANY CONSIDER IT THE ULTIMATE PRAIRIE HOUSE.

Wright's last great Prairie House, and perhaps the most dramatic of all, was the Robie House. The long, low red brick house was built in Chicago between 1907 and 1909. Locals nicknamed it "The Battleship." When Frederick Robie, a bicycle manufacturer, came to Wright, he knew exactly what he wanted. "I wanted rooms without interruptions," he said. "I wanted the windows without curvature and doodads inside and out."

Wright gave Robie exactly what he wanted—an astounding work of art. He designed all the furniture "as a natural part of the building." The chairs grouped around the dining table form a room within a room, an idea he had used in his house at Oak Park. But even Wright admitted his chairs weren't comfortable. Once he remarked, "I have been black and blue in some spot, somewhere, almost all my life from too much intimate contact with my own early furniture." The total cost of the Robie House, including the custom-made furnishings, came in at $59,000, a thousand under budget. In those days, the average middle-class house cost about $5,000 to build. Robie was willing to spend much more and was delighted with his new home.

At forty-two, Wright was a success. He had built more than one hundred and fifty structures but he still didn't have the recognition and acceptance he craved. Many Americans regarded his buildings as odd and too unusual. When he received an invitation from the firm of Ernst Wasmuth in Berlin to publish a complete monograph of his work, Wright was tempted to leave Oak Park and go to Germany where his modern ideas would be appreciated. Despite his success, debts plagued him and he was always short of cash. Clients often didn't pay their bills on time and Wright had a big family to support and salaries to pay. After working hard for so many years, he was burned out.

In his autobiography he wrote, "I was losing my grip on my work and even my interest in it. . . . What I wanted I did not know. I loved my children. I loved my home. A true home is the finest ideal of man, and yet—well, to gain freedom I asked for a divorce."

Kitty refused. She loved her husband dearly and hoped he would change his mind. But Wright's attachment to Mamah Cheney had grown too strong.

In the fall of 1909 Wright sold many of his Japanese prints to raise money and took a train to New York. There he rendezvoused with Mamah and they sailed for Europe. Wright left behind his wife, children, mother, a flourishing practice of architecture, and a $900 grocer's bill.

IN

WRIGHT HAD DEVOTED HIS life to architecture. Now at age forty-two he had no home of his own, no clients, no buildings to build. He and Mamah traveled from Germany to Italy, and Wright turned to writing and making a book. The stunning *Wasmuth Portfolio*, published in 1910, showed drawings and floor plans of all of his work. Architecture students in

CHAPTER FIVE

Europe used it as a textbook.

Back in the United States, Wright's wife, Kitty, also made a book. She still loved her husband and while he was gone she put together *Daily Reminders*. Each page marked a day of that difficult year with a poem, photo, or magazine illustration. Kitty saved the book for her husband in

EXILE

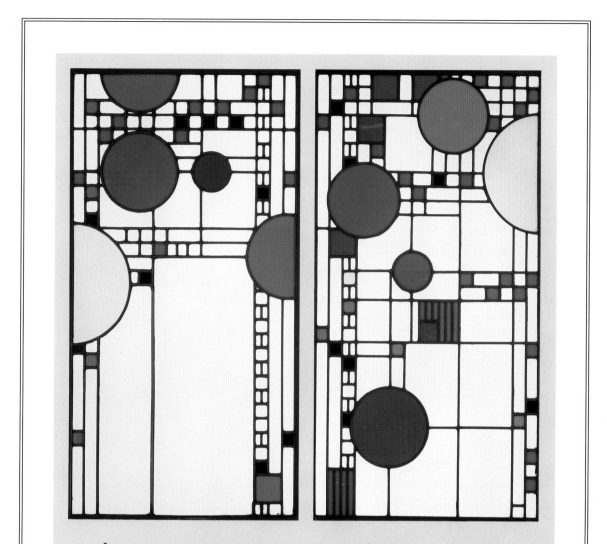

IN DESIGNING THESE WINDOWS FOR THE COONLEY PLAYHOUSE,
WRIGHT WAS INSPIRED BY A PARADE ON A NATIONAL HOLIDAY. AFTER
THE PARADE HE BROUGHT A BUNCH OF GAS-FILLED BALLOONS TO HIS
OFFICE AND STUDIED THE WAY THEY BOBBED UP AND DOWN.

(Following page) TALIESIN HOUSE IS REFLECTED IN THE POND.
THIS PLACE HAS BEEN DESCRIBED AS ONE OF THE MOST BEAUTIFUL
SPOTS ON EARTH. HERE WRIGHT CREATED A PERFECT HARMONY
OF LANDSCAPE AND ARCHITECTURE—A NATURAL HOUSE.

the hope that he would eventually return to her.

Wright did return to Chicago. He remodeled his studio in Oak Park as living quarters for Kitty and the children, though he took his own apartment downtown. Many people disapproved of Wright's behavior as a family man and snubbed him. Even his few loyal friends criticized him. One of them commented that Wright now looked like the man on the Quaker Oats package with his "knee trousers, long stockings, broad-brimmed brown hat, and lordly strut."

Wright needed a refuge, and his mother came to the rescue. She bought some land near the family farm in Spring Green, Wisconsin, and gave it to Wright. There he designed a home where he and Mamah Cheney could begin a new life—the ultimate natural house, blending landscape and architecture. Wright planned the estate as a working farm as well as a home, office, and studio-workshop. He wanted to grow his own fruits and vegetables and raise livestock. With characteristic humor he named the pigpen area Pork Avenue.

Wright called the entire estate Taliesin (Tal/ee/essen), which means "shining brow" in Welsh. Indeed, the house runs along the hillside like the ridge of a brow on a forehead. When he was a boy, this site had been one of his favorite places to gather wildflowers. "It was unthinkable to me," he wrote, "at least unbearable, that any house should be put *on* that beloved hill. I knew well that no house should ever be *on* a hill or *on* anything. It should be *of* the hill . . . belong to the hill, as trees and the ledges or rock did."

Wright built with local materials—sand from the banks of the Wisconsin River for mixing plaster and limestone quarried a mile away for building walls. He instructed the masons to set the stones in overlapping ledges, the way they form naturally in the quarry.

Stone steps led to flower gardens and courtyards. Each court contained a fountain and piece of Oriental art. More sculptures, urns, and screens decorated the rooms inside, warmed in winter by rugged stone fireplaces. Wright planned the house so that the sun came through the windows into every room at some time during the day. Corner windows, called mitered windows, were sealed with a clear adhesive and provided uninterrupted views of the treetops and pond. Casement windows, Wright's favorite, swung open to let in "the perfume of the blossoms and the songs of the birds." During the winter months, icicles hung from the eaves, transforming Taliesin into a "frosted palace."

Wright and Mamah Cheney moved in just before Christmas 1911 and lived there for three years. Her children visited every summer. Edwin Cheney had agreed to a divorce, but Kitty still refused to give one to Wright. Some of Wright's children missed their father, others felt angry.

Wright missed his family, too. Whenever he went to his Chicago office he visited Oak Park. He would go to his house after dark and stand outside, listening to his children's voices through the half-open windows, reassuring himself that they were all right.

Throughout these years Wright lost most of his old clients. A few faithful friends gave him work. The Coonleys, for instance, asked him to build a school in Riverside, Illinois. It was called a Playhouse because the children learned history by writing and performing plays about historical events. For this, Wright designed a stage and art glass windows with balloons, flags, and confetti.

Since most people lost faith in him as a family man and no longer trusted him to design their homes, Wright looked for different kinds of challenging projects. He heard about a commission for designing a new Imperial Hotel in Tokyo, Japan, and was eager to land the job. Friends helped him make contacts and, in 1913, he and Mamah traveled to Tokyo. Wright drew rough sketches and preliminary plans and started discussing arrangements with the hotel company. He then went back to Taliesin and made more drawings and models for the new hotel.

This project was temporarily interrupted by another stimulating challenge. Ed Waller, the son of one of Wright's first clients, asked Wright to create an indoor/outdoor entertainment center for dinner, dancing, and concerts on the south side of Chicago. It was called Midway Gardens. One weekend, Wright visualized the entire project before ever setting a pencil to paper. "The thing had simply shaken itself out of my sleeve," he wrote in his autobiography. Wright designed everything—from the tables, chairs, and chinaware down to decorative sculptures and murals. Assisted by his son John, Wright commuted between Chicago and Spring Green while Midway Gardens was under construction.

One day while supervising a mural that John was painting, Wright received a phone call. The news was terrible. Taliesin was on fire. He and John dashed to the station and took the first train to Spring Green. Reporters were on board. So was Edwin Cheney. Along the way reporters told them horrible news.

A new chef and handyman had gone mad and set fire to the house, then barred the doors and brutally murdered Mamah and her children. As the other lunch guests tried to escape and jump out the windows, he attacked them, too. Four more people later died of wounds and burns. John said he never forgot the look of anguish on his father's face as he learned the ghastly details. Wright and Cheney silently clasped hands in mutual grief and despair.

Cheney took the bodies of his children home. The other victims were buried by their families. At Taliesin, Wright had a plain casket made for Mamah. He filled it with flowers cut from her garden and buried her himself.

Wright missed Mamah dreadfully and lost weight at first. He may even have begun to change his birth date at this point and borrowed hers, 1869, as a way of remembering her. Only work comforted him. He busied himself with the task of rebuilding Taliesin and continued with the Imperial Hotel project.

FRANK LLOYD WRIGHT LIVED AND WORKED WITH HIS APPRENTICES AT TALIESIN. THERE WERE NO FORMAL LECTURES OR CLASSES. YOUNG STUDENTS LEARNED BY PARTICIPATING IN HIS PROJECTS.

WRIGHT WANTED THE IMPERIAL HOTEL TO BLEND IN WITH ITS SURROUNDINGS. HE USED LOCAL MATERIALS SUCH AS *OYA* AND LAVA STONE IN CONSTRUCTION.

Meanwhile, World War I broke out. Wright was a pacifist like his Unitarian relatives and opposed the war. He spent the war years preoccupied with work.

Shortly after the tragedy at Taliesin, Wright received a sympathetic letter from someone he had never met. Her name was Miriam Noel. She was a sophisticated, stylish divorcée who had lived in Paris and fancied herself a sculptress. Wright was charmed by her note and arranged to meet her. Soon they were romantically involved and he moved her to Taliesin, along with his mother. In 1916, after he was officially hired as the architect of the new Imperial Hotel, he sailed to Japan with Miriam and began construction.

The hotel was to be a comfortable place where foreigners could stay. Wright wanted to give Japan the best of Western technology, while still respecting its traditions. His biggest concern, however, was earthquakes.

In Tokyo, Wright tested his theories about earthquake-proof foundations. "Why fight the quake?" he asked. "Why not sympathize with it and outwit it?" After collecting data and making calculations with his son, John, and Paul Mueller, a builder who had worked on Midway Gardens, he came up with an idea. He would "float" the hotel foundation on the mud beneath the ground surface, using the cantilever principle. The weight of the floor and roof would be supported in the center, balanced the way "a waiter carries a tray on his upraised arm and fingers." He planned a large pool in the entrance court to serve both as an architectural feature and as an independent water supply in case of fire. He remembered only too well the fire at Taliesin.

As work progressed on the hotel, rumors spread that Wright was crazy. In the event of an earthquake, the new building would collapse and sink into the mud. He ignored the rumors and forged ahead with designs for furniture, upholstery, rugs, and dinnerware. The work was very hard and went on for six years.

An added difficulty was Wright's personal life. His relationship with Miriam Noel soured. She was a moody woman, addicted to alcohol and drugs and given to "frequent outbreaks." The stress this created for Wright, in addition to the hardships of building the hotel, made him physically ill. So his mother, now in her eighties, sailed to Japan to take care of him.

One of the construction problems he was struggling with concerned the courtyard pool. The building committee wanted to save money by eliminating it. Wright argued that the water would be necessary if the city water supply was cut off after a quake. As if on cue—an earthquake struck! Chimneys fell off the old Imperial Hotel, but the new one was undamaged. "The work had been proved," Wright said, and the committee agreed to put in the pool.

A year later, in 1923, while in Los Angeles, he heard that Japan had been hit by a terrible earthquake. The Kanto earthquake was the worst natural disaster in recorded history at that time. According to the first reports, Tokyo had been wiped out. Wright received a call informing him that the Imperial Hotel was totally destroyed. But he didn't believe it. A week later he received a telegram from a friend and representative of the Imperial household. It read:

FOLLOWING WIRELESS RECEIVED TODAY FROM TOKYO, HOTEL STANDS UNDAMAGED AS MONUMENT TO YOUR GENIUS HUNDREDS OF HOMELESS PROVIDED BY PERFECTLY MAINTAINED SERVICE CONGRATULATIONS.

As letters arrived, Wright was relieved to hear that nearly all his friends were safe. In a gratifying postscript, he learned that after the quake, when fire swept across the city, hotel boys formed a bucket brigade at the courtyard pool—the only water supply available anywhere. That was what saved the Imperial Hotel from burning down.

During these years, Wright traveled back and forth across the Pacific. In California, he worked with some new clients. Aline Barnsdall was an oil heiress who was passionately interested in the theater. She wanted Wright to create a colony for her on Olive Hill in Los Angeles that would include theaters, residences for actors, shops, and her own home. Only her house was built.

Barnsdall named it Hollyhock House after her favorite flower and it has been compared to a fortress or Mayan temple. Wright transformed the hollyhock into an abstract geometric motif and integrated it into the structure of the concrete columns, piers, art glass doors and windows, and wooden dining chairs.

He used a different building technique for Alice Millard, another client, from Highland Park, Illinois. Now Millard wanted something in Pasadena, California, appropriate for the landscape, climate, and her collection of antique books. La Miniatura, the house Wright built for her in 1923, was his first entirely concrete block house. Since he sited it in a ravine filled with eucalyptus, he gave the blocks a surface pattern that blended with the trees.

Wright had been experimenting with the concrete block as a building material. "It was the cheapest (and ugliest) thing in the building world," he wrote. "Why not see what could be done with that gutter rat?" With his oldest son, Lloyd, also an architect, he invented a new system. He used hollow, precast concrete blocks that were plain, perforated, or patterned and strung them through with steel rods, then filled them where necessary with poured concrete. Wright thought of the process as weaving and considered the resulting wall surface a kind of textile. Therefore, he called his new system "textile block construction."

Between 1923 and 1924, Wright built three more block-system houses in the Hollywood Hills for John Storer, Charles Ennis, and Samuel Freeman.

The Storer House is two stories high and features exciting split-levels inside. The living room is on the upper level and opens onto terraces. The Ennis House is the largest and most monumental. A long colonnaded gallery leads from the dining room to three small bedrooms. From the gallery, steps lead up to the dining room, half a level above the living room. Here again, Wright played with split-levels. In the Freeman House, floor-to-ceiling windows in the upper-level living room offer breathtaking views of Hollywood below. Perforated blocks allow natural light to come through and lowered ceilings near the central fireplace create intimate seating areas.

Despite the many good points of the textile block houses, they proved to be impractical. They were difficult and expensive to build. The blocks took too long to make and set in place. They crumbled easily and absorbed rainwater and smog. Since the Californians didn't want any more of them, Wright returned to Taliesin.

As in California, there were no more commissions for Wright in the Midwest. Young Chicago architects rejected the Prairie House after World War I and went "Classic." So Wright took up writing and published technical articles about constructing the Imperial Hotel. It is said that he spent his entire earnings from the hotel project on buying more Japanese art for his extensive collection.

At age fifty-seven, more than a decade after he had left Oak Park, Wright once again had few clients, little cash, and big debts. Although he had a home, it seemed empty. His first wife, Kitty, finally divorced him in 1922. Then his mother died in February 1923. Shortly after, Wright married Miriam Noel to stabilize their relationship, but a few months later she left him. He wrote to his son Lloyd: "I don't know where to turn at present but I know I've got to work. . . . That's all I ever really know."

FLOOR-TO-CEILING WINDOWS AND GLASS DOORS IN THE FREEMAN HOUSE LOOK OUT TOWARD HOLLYWOOD, CALIFORNIA. SAMUEL FREEMAN SAID, "WHEN THE HOUSE WAS FINISHED ENOUGH SO WE COULD MOVE IN, WE DID NOT HAVE A STICK OF FURNITURE. WE SAT ON BOXES, AND THE HOUSE NEVER SEEMED BARE."

The Guggenheim Museum and the Art of this Century

WRIGHT CHOSE THE SPIRAL RAMP FOR THE GUGGENHEIM MUSEUM BECAUSE
HE FELT VISITORS COULD VIEW ART MORE COMFORTABLY WALKING ALONG
AN AIRY OPEN SPACE, RATHER THAN THROUGH STUFFY GALLERIES.

A Promise

I N N O V E M B E R , 1 9 2 4 , W R I G H T met a beautiful young woman named Olgivanna Hinzenberg, and his life changed. By the first of the new year they were living together at Taliesin. He was fifty-seven, and she was twenty-six.

Olgivanna had been married before and had a daughter who stayed

Chapter Six

with her and Wright. In the spring Olgivanna became pregnant and Wright was delighted. The future looked wonderful until a fire broke out in a bedroom at Taliesin one evening. Wright organized a bucket brigade but high winds fanned the flames and the fire spread beneath the roof. Wright climbed to "the smoking roofs . . . and fought" to save the work-

Kept

rooms. A sudden rainstorm put out the fire just as it reached the studio-workshop, but the living quarters and Wright's collection of Oriental art objects were destroyed. Wright was then again pinched for money. "My Tokyo earnings all went up in smoke," he said. "All I could show for my work and wanderings in the Orient for years past were the leather trousers, burned socks, and shirt in which I now stood defeated."

MRS. FRANK LLOYD WRIGHT IN THE LOGGIA, 1936. LIKE THE BUDDHA ON THE WALL, OLGIVANNA SERENELY GRACES TALIESIN.

However, Wright still had many of his prints safely stored in the vault. He had a good eye and had collected hundreds of museum-quality wood-block prints by Japanese masters. He even owned and saved ten original woodblocks of the artist Ando Hiroshige and was one of three people outside of Japan known to have them. Yet Wright couldn't sell the art for what it was worth because the market had declined and values dropped.

So Wright borrowed money from the bank and from friends, using his print collection as collateral, and he optimistically drew plans for Taliesin III. In July he filed for divorce from Miriam Noel and then his real troubles began. She sued him for money and property and hounded him for years. After Olgivanna gave birth to a daughter in December 1925, Wright went into hiding upon advice from his lawyer, and his new "little family" stayed on the move.

The following October, Miriam went so far as to have Wright arrested for transporting Olgivanna, an unmarried woman, across state lines. Wright spent two miserable nights in jail but took advantage of the opportunity to size up the terrible architecture. He appeared in county and municipal courts and posted bonds to get out of jail. Sensational publicity kept clients away and prevented him from doing the one thing he wanted to do—work.

The worst moment came when the bank threatened to take Taliesin away from him. Finally a settlement was made with the bank and Wright went home with his family. After his divorce from Miriam became final in 1928, he married Olgivanna. Now he was ready to go back to work on projects started during these difficult years.

In the late 1920s, Wright did little actual building. The few commissions he received were not executed, usually for lack of funds. Yet Wright

THIS DRAWING GIVES A NIGHT VIEW OF THE TWIN CANTILEVERED BRIDGES PROJECT FOR PITTSBURGH. HERE WRIGHT SHOWED WHAT COULD BE DONE WITH STEEL. "THE STEEL STRAND IS A MARVEL," HE SAID, "A MIRACLE OF STRENGTH FOR ITS WEIGHT AND COST."

believed that his unbuilt projects were his most interesting.

Sugarloaf Mountain in Frederick County, Maryland, was planned as a tourist attraction, with a planetarium, restaurant, movie theater, and observation decks. Here Wright designed his first spiral ramp for cars and later used it as a walkway in the Guggenheim Museum in New York.

Steel Cathedral was to have been over two thousand feet high, making it the largest church in the world, big enough to seat a million people. The Empire State Building would have fit inside. Later Wright reduced and refined the tepeelike design for Beth Sholom Synagogue in Elkins Park, Pennsylvania.

Wright was fascinated by the materials of glass and steel. He called steel "the most significant material of this age" because of its strength, cheapness and tenuity, or quality of pull. "The spiderweb is a good inspiration for steel construction," Wright said. The steel strands in the drawing *Twin Cantilevered Bridges Project for Pittsburgh* look like membranes of a spider's web.

Wright expanded this image when discussing the potential of glass. "Why not

THE DRAFTING ROOM AT HILLSIDE WAS ADDED IN 1938.
WRIGHT CALLED IT "THE ABSTRACT FOREST" BECAUSE OF THE
INTRICATE TRUSS WORK OF OAK BEAMS.

now combine it with steel, the spider's web . . . and make it the building itself?" Technology had made glass cheap and available as never before, and Wright envisioned modern cities with luminous "glass and bronze" buildings.

When he stayed in New York, Wright had a chance to observe urban problems of overcrowding, traffic, and pollution. In a project for the pastor of St. Mark's-in-the-Bouwerie, in New York, he designed three apartment towers with outer walls of glass set into copper frames. To make the towers secure, Wright proposed the taproot principle of construction he had used in building the Romeo and Juliet windmill. Later on he used the design to build his New York skyscraper as the tower for H. C. Price Company in Bartlesville, Oklahoma.

Then, in 1927, Wright discovered the desert. He was asked to design a large resort, the San-Marcos-in-the-Desert in Chandler, Arizona, and fell in love with the site. He studied the tall saguaro cactus for inspiration and excitedly began making sketches.

While working on the project, Wright built his first campsite—Ocatillo, named for another plant. Just as he was about to start construction on the hotel in 1929, the stock market crashed. The client had no money to complete the project, so Wright left Arizona and drove back to Wisconsin.

During the Depression years when Wright had no commissions, he did more writing and lecturing. *An Autobiography* was published in 1932. Many aspiring architects read it and wrote to him asking if they could study with him.

In the fall of that same year, Wright opened a School of the Allied Arts, called the Fellowship, on the old Hillside Home School property his aunts had left him when they died. He followed their educational tradition of learning by doing.

For $650 tuition, young people studied music, dancing, weaving, and, of course, architecture, and also spent a certain number of hours every day farming, taking care of the livestock, cooking, repairing roads, and constructing buildings. In the drafting room the apprentices assisted Wright with his projects and worked on their own designs.

Critics said Wright formed the school to support his practice, grow his food, and run his estate. Yet applicants kept coming and had to be turned away or go on a waiting list, even when tuition was raised to $1,100. Wright worked alongside his "boys and girls" as they built living quarters, a new drafting room, and a playhouse.

At the playhouse, Wright showed foreign films to the public every Sunday for an admission price of fifty cents, which included tea afterward. Wright loved movies, especially Westerns and Charlie Chaplin comedies. In later years, the routine changed and the entire Fellowship saw movies on Saturday nights and went on picnics on Sundays.

In those days Wright sported a cape (to make him look taller), shoes with elevated heels, tweed trousers fastened at the ankles with cloth ties (to keep out drafts), and a beret, porkpie hat, or sombrero. When out driving he wore an aviator's cap.

Wright adored cars and every model he had was painted Cherokee red. With his extraordinary vision he foresaw the increase of cars and highways in America and wanted to make gas stations attractive as well as functional.

In 1932, he designed a service station with overhead fuel lines, a second-floor waiting room, and a cantilevered canopy extending out from the walls. The design was adapted and finally built in 1956 by R. W. Lindholm in Cloquet, Minnesota. The townspeople were so proud of the only Frank Lloyd Wright–designed service station in America that when they thought it would be torn down to make room for a new highway, they had the highway built around it.

The Standardized Overhead Service Station was originally intended as part of Broadacre City, a scale model of an ideal community that Wright planned with his apprentices. The model was first exhibited in New York and then traveled throughout the United States.

Edgar J. Kaufmann, the father of one of the apprentices, financed the traveling exhibit. In 1935, he asked Wright to design a weekend house for him on wooded family land in Bear Run, Pennsylvania. Kaufmann wanted to have a view of a waterfall on the property. Wright had a different idea. When they looked over the land together to choose a building site, Wright said, "E. J., where do you like to sit?" Kaufmann pointed to a big rock overlooking the waterfall—and Wright made that spot the hearthstone of the house. He wanted his client to live over the waterfall, not just look at it.

The day Kaufmann came to Taliesin to see the first plans for the house, there weren't any. To the amazement of the apprentices standing by, Wright made the first drawings with colored pencils in a couple of hours while Kaufmann was en route. "The design just poured out of him," Edgar Tafel recalled. The drawings

FALLINGWATER IS A TRULY NATURAL HOUSE. WRIGHT SAID, "YOU LISTEN TO FALLINGWATER THE WAY YOU LISTEN TO THE QUIET OF THE COUNTRY."

PICTURED HERE IN THE WINTERTIME IS FALLINGWATER.
IN ANY SEASON THE HOUSE SEEMS TO BLEND WITH THE SURROUNDING
WOODS AND CLIFFS.

were finished minutes before Kaufmann arrived. After he saw them, Kaufmann said, "Don't change a thing." And Wright didn't.

Wright named the house Fallingwater. The living room is cantilevered right over the waterfall like a diving board. Suspended stairs lead from the living room down to the stream. The whole house is a series of reinforced concrete trays anchored to a tall stone core. Wright said the house showed how "buildings grow from their sites." He used stone from a local quarry for the chimney and floors and tinted the poured concrete a shade of apricot to harmonize with the surrounding foliage.

Fallingwater became one of the most famous private houses of the twentieth century. The American Institute of Architects (AIA) has designated it as one of seventeen buildings designed by Wright to be preserved as examples of his contribution to American culture.

In 1936, Wright created another landmark structure, the Johnson Wax Administration Building in Racine, Wisconsin. The central open work space featured unusual columns that look like giant mushrooms or lily pads. At first the Industrial Commission wouldn't give him a permit for the columns. Wright proved they could stand by having one column poured, propped up, then loaded with three times its required weight. The props were removed and the column remained standing. The permit was issued. When the building opened, it was a sensation.

There was only one problem. Wright had designed his own streamlined steel furniture, and his three-legged chair tipped like the suicide chair he had invented for the Larkin Building. Many employees and visitors fell off. When the president of the company asked him why he hadn't designed four legs on the chair, Wright replied, "You won't tip if you sit back and put your two feet on the ground because then you've got five legs holding you up. If five legs won't hold you, then I don't know what will!"

Wright didn't limit himself to startling office buildings and impressive country houses. One of his main concerns had always been low-cost housing for middle-income families. In the 1930s, he came up with a concept called the Usonian House.

Wright coined the word *Usonian* to mean a reformed American society. Usonian houses were intended to offer handsome economical dwellings for an informal way of life without servants. The first one was built in 1936 for Herbert Jacobs, a newspaper reporter in Madison, Wisconsin. It was 1,500 square feet and cost $5,500, including the architect's fee.

The one-story house introduced features found in all of the Usonian homes: a bedroom zone with small sleeping spaces; a large living room with a dining area or table near the kitchen instead of a formal dining room; built-in furniture, open shelves, and indirect lighting; radiant heating (pipe coils laid in the foundation underneath the concrete floor); high clerestory windows running under the roof overhang; and a carport at the entrance to replace a garage.

The Usonian houses were made with board and batten construction; that is, ready-made units that could efficiently be put together. By using glass, wood, brick, and stone, both on the inside and the outside, Wright eliminated the need for paint, varnish, wallpaper, and wall decoration. The houses were easy to maintain and provided the occupants

WORKERS SIT AT METAL DESKS DESIGNED BY WRIGHT FOR THE JOHNSON WAX ADMINISTRATION BUILDING IN RACINE, WISCONSIN.

IN THE LOREN POPE HOUSE
(THE POPE-LEIGHY HOUSE) LIGHT
COMES THROUGH CLERESTORY
WINDOWS DECORATED WITH A
PUNCHED-OUT DESIGN.

with varied spaces and ever-changing vistas. Loren Pope said of his house in Falls Church, Virginia, "The house gives you a sense of protection, but never of being closed in."

Wright designed more than one hundred of these modest, modern-looking houses for clients throughout America. Robert Berger, a schoolteacher in northern California, built his home himself to save money. After it was finished, his twelve-year-old son, Jim, sent a letter to Wright asking him to design a matching doghouse for his Labrador retriever, Eddie. Wright sketched a design on the back of an envelope and eventually drew up plans. Jim and his father built the doghouse, but Eddie didn't like it and refused to go in it.

In 1937, after Wright recovered from pneumonia, he bought land in Scottsdale, Arizona, and moved the whole Fellowship there for the winter months. It became a permanent second home and was named Taliesin West. Wright designed the living quarters and workroom in triangular shapes, repeating the forms of the distant mountains. White canvas stretched over the redwood frames. Desert stones and bits of Oriental art were embedded in concrete walls.

An art museum was Wright's next major project. In 1943, Solomon Guggenheim, an industrialist and patron of the arts, asked Wright to design a museum in New York for his collection of twentieth-century nonobjective art. Nonobjective art was a movement started by Wassily Kandinsky, who painted explosive, colorful abstractions that did not depict or represent anything seen in reality. Wright matched this highly imaginative art with an unusual solution for the form of the museum.

Wright wanted to design "one great space on a single continuous floor," so he twisted a long gallery around a central well. The exterior shape of a reinforced concrete spiral growing larger toward the top expresses the inner space. At the ground level there is room for an airy entryway, sculpture garden, and parking.

Inside, a magnificent domed skylight and window slits under the ramp provide natural light for viewing the paintings in their true colors. Walls slope away

TALIESIN WEST EMERGES NATURALLY FROM THE DESERT FLOOR.
THE TRIANGULAR TRUSSES ARE MADE OF REDWOOD.

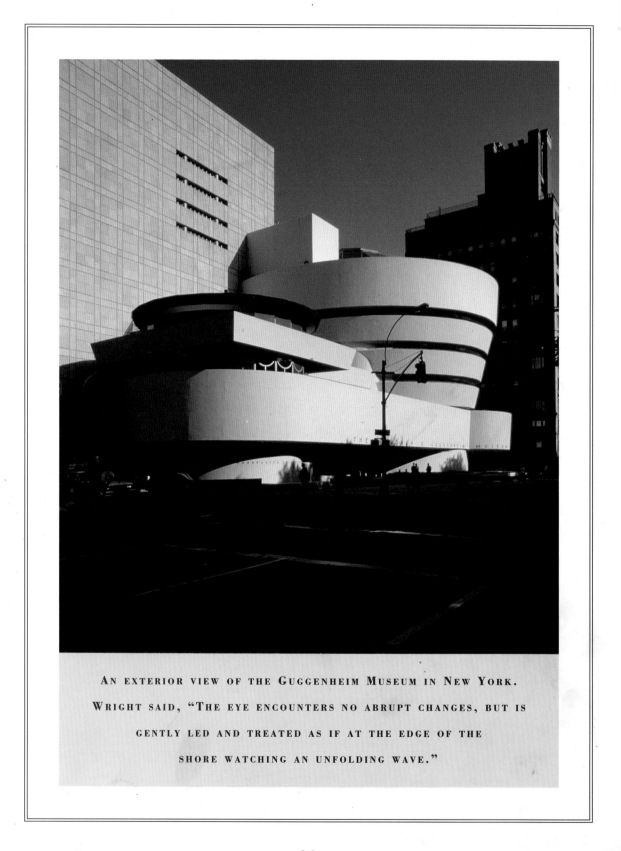

AN EXTERIOR VIEW OF THE GUGGENHEIM MUSEUM IN NEW YORK.
WRIGHT SAID, "THE EYE ENCOUNTERS NO ABRUPT CHANGES, BUT IS
GENTLY LED AND TREATED AS IF AT THE EDGE OF THE
SHORE WATCHING AN UNFOLDING WAVE."

from the floors at approximately the angle at which a canvas tilts on an easel. Twenty-one artists objected at first to having their work shown on walls slant- ed outward. And some viewers found it hard to stand on a slanted ramp and view the art on tilted walls. But most people enjoyed the experience of riding an ele- vator to the highest level of the ramp, then walking down around an open court, moving in a single direction in "a quiet unbroken wave." Wright saw the ramp as "space in motion." He compared the air-conditioned chambers in which the paintings would be shown to "chambers something like those of 'the chambered nau- tilus,'" a spiral seashell in his own collection.

Wright's daring design sparked a long series of controversies. Critics said it looked like a wash- ing machine on Fifth Avenue. As planning went on during World War II, costs of materials and labor rose, building codes changed, and construction was delayed. But Guggenheim loved the plan and thought it was a masterpiece; he

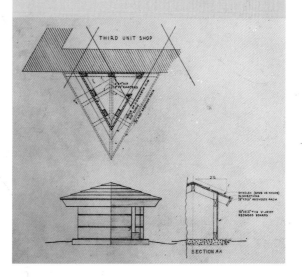

A PLAN AND ELEVATION OF THE BERGER USONIAN DOGHOUSE, THE ONLY DOGHOUSE WRIGHT EVER DESIGNED. THE TRIANGULAR SHAPE MATCHES THE TRIANGULAR SHAPE OF THE FAMILY'S HOUSE.

even set aside money in his will for the museum before he died in 1949.

That same year Wright received a gold medal from the AIA. Although Wright had never joined the organization because he felt the AIA had overlooked and neglected him, now he was pleased to finally be recognized by his peers. More medals, awards, exhibitions of his work, and honorary degrees soon followed.

One of the most precious to him was an honorary Doctorate of Fine Arts from the University of Wisconsin. For years Wright had felt embarrassed by his lack of formal education and he treasured this belated degree.

As honors multiplied, so did commissions. Wright's last years were his busiest. In 1956 he was asked to design a television antenna for Chicago that would be one mile high. Wright decided to put an office building beneath the antenna and so came up with his ultimate skyscraper, Mile High. Some people thought the plan was amusing, others thought Wright was crazy, but he had all the details worked out—from the atomic-powered elevators to parking ramps for fifteen thousand cars and the landing decks for seventy-five helicopters.

SINCE DAVID WRIGHT WAS IN THE CONCRETE MASONRY BUSINESS, HE WANTED TO DEMONSTRATE WHAT COULD BE DONE WITH THIS BUILDING MATERIAL. THE CURVED PHILIPPINE MAHOGANY CEILING IN HIS HOUSE OFFERS A WARM CONTRAST TO THE CONCRETE BLOCKS.

From 1948 to 1950, while he was working on the Guggenheim Museum, he explored spirals and circular shapes in the V. C. Morris Shop in San Francisco, California. The shop originally sold fine glassware and silver. To contrast it with other stores on the street and to call attention to it, Wright built a plain brick outer wall with an arched opening similar to the one in the Dana House. The interior of the Morris

Shop has a ramp spiraling to the second floor and portholes displaying gifts.

Wright continued his experiments with circular shapes when he designed a house for his son David in Phoenix, Arizona. The cement-block house coils around a garden and a ramp leads to the front door. Within, curved fireplaces, curved corridors, and round windows repeat the theme. Wright designed a bold area rug with a pattern of intersecting circles and curved furniture. The house is near Taliesin West and Wright frequently dropped by (to the annoyance of David and his wife), and rearranged furniture. Wright's youngest son, Llewellyn, commented, "I think he always did indeed feel that any house he had designed still belonged to him." Wright liked David's house so much that he gave it his special seal of approval—a square red signature tile reserved for only a few of his buildings. He inscribed his initials, FLLW, with a long tail or slash on the W, in the unbaked clay.

As Wright got older, his ideas grew more imaginative. One of his last projects, the Broadacre City Project, was a design for transportation of the future—an atomic-powered car and a helicopter taxi shaped like a spinning top. Up until the end, Wright dreamed of an ideal city and an educational system that would produce citizens who would demand good architecture. "I dreamed at sixteen of building secure against earthquake—I have done so now," he said. "I dreamed of building tall—I can now build a mile high . . . and I can 'build houses to fit people' . . . a promise kept, a prophecy fulfilled."

Frank Lloyd Wright died in April 1959, a few months before the Guggenheim Museum opened, at the age of ninety-one. The museum immediately became a major New York attraction. Then, from 1989 to 1992, it was closed for renovations and expansion. The new commissioned architects attempted to remain true to Wright's original vision. Would he have approved?

Once he told his apprentices, "When you are truly creative in your attempt to design, this thing that we call good design begins and never has an end."

LIST OF ILLUSTRATIONS

Pages 42–43: Frank Lloyd Wright's house. 1889–1909. Photograph: Jon Miller/Hedrich-Blessing, Chicago

Page 45: Romeo and Juliet Windmill. 1896. The State Historical Society of Wisconsin, Iconographic Collections, Madison (WHi X3 23632, lot 2312)

Pages 46–47: Winslow House. The Frank Lloyd Wright Foundation, Scottsdale, Arizona (#9305.013). © The Frank Lloyd Wright Foundation

Page 49: Susan Lawrence Dana House. 1902. Illinois Historic Preservation Agency, Springfield, Illinois. Photograph: © 1990 Doug Carr

Page 52: Larkin Building, interior, view from balcony. 1904–5; demolished 1946. The Frank Lloyd Wright Foundation, Scottsdale, Arizona (#0403.0058)

Page 53: Larkin Building, armchair. c. 1904. Painted steel with original leather-covered seat, casters, 38 x 24½ x 21". Photograph: © 1994 Thomas A. Heinz

Page 54: Unity Temple. 1905–7. Chicago Historical Society. Photograph: Hedrich-Blessing, Chicago

Page 55: Unity Temple, interior view. 1905–7. Photograph: © 1994 Thomas A. Heinz

Pages 56–57: The Coonley House, view of the living room. c. 1910. The Frank Lloyd Wright Foundation, Scottsdale, Arizona (#0803.023)

Page 58: Frederick C. Robie House. Ink drawing from *Wasmuth Portfolio*. Chicago, Illinois. The Frank Lloyd Wright Foundation, Scottsdale, Arizona (#0908.005). © Frank Lloyd Wright Foundation

Page 61: Coonley Playhouse windows. 1912. Leaded clear and cased glass, each 18⅝ x 34³/₁₆". The Museum of Modern Art, New York, Joseph H. Heil Fund

Page 62: Taliesin House, lake elevation. Spring Green, Wisconsin. 1927. Photograph: © 1994 Thomas A. Heinz

Page 65: Frank Lloyd Wright and apprentices. 1937. Chicago Historical Society. Photograph: Hedrich-Blessing, Chicago (HB-44414-H)

Page 66: Imperial Hotel, exterior with pool in foreground. 1915 (demolished) rebuilt. Photograph: © 1994 Thomas A. Heinz

Pages 70–71: Samuel Freeman House, interior, view looking towards Hollywood. 1923. Photograph: Julius Shulman, Los Angeles

Page 72: Interior view of the Solomon R. Guggenheim Museum. Photograph: David Heald, © The Solomon R. Guggenheim Foundation, New York

Page 74: Mrs. Frank Lloyd Wright. 1936. Photograph: Edmund Teske

Page 75: Night view of Twin Cantilevered Bridges Project. 1948. Tempera on illustration board. The Frank Lloyd Wright Foundation, Scottsdale, Arizona (#4836.009). © The Frank Lloyd Wright Foundation

Page 76: The Hillside Home School, drafting room. 1938. Photograph: Edmund Teske

Page 79: Edgar J. Kaufmann House, "Fallingwater," perspective drawing. 1935. Pencil and color pencil on tracing paper, 33 x 17". The Frank Lloyd Wright Foundation, Scottsdale, Arizona (#3602.004). © The Frank Lloyd Wright Foundation

Page 80: Edgar J. Kaufmann House, "Fallingwater," exterior. 1935. Photograph: © 1994 Thomas A. Heinz

Pages 82–83: S. C. Johnson Wax Company Administration Building. Photograph: S. C. Johnson Wax, Racine

Page 84: Loren Pope (Pope-Leighy House). 1939. (Relocated to Mount Vernon, Virginia, in 1964.) Photograph: © 1994 Thomas A. Heinz

Page 85: Taliesin West, exterior. 1937. Photograph: © 1994 Thomas A. Heinz

Page 86: The Solomon R. Guggenheim Museum. Photograph: © 1994 Thomas A. Heinz

Page 87: Mr. and Mrs. Robert Berger Doghouse. 1950. Pencil on tracing paper. The Frank Lloyd Wright Foundation, Scottsdale, Arizona (#5039.003). © The Frank Lloyd Wright Foundation

Page 88: David S. Wright House. 1950. Photograph: J. Spencer Lake, San Diego

Index